Daasy Agnes

A Memoir by Dorothy Burgard

Water Color llustrations by Dorothy Burgard

authorHOUSE™

1663 LIBERTY DRIVE, SUITE 200
BLOOMINGTON, INDIANA 47403
(800) 839-8640
WWW.AUTHORHOUSE.COM

First published by AuthorHouse 02/12/05

ISBN: 1-4208-2001-X (sc)

Library of Congress Control Number: 2005902234

Printed in the United States of America
Bloomington, Indiana

This book is printed on acid-free paper.

Acknowledgements

I would like to express my gratitude to my daughter Judy Heiser for all the time she spent typing this story, to my son Joseph Burgard for editing this book, and to my daughter-in-law Suzie Kirrane for her work on the book layout. This book would not have been possible without all of their help.

Sweet Memories

How well I remember childhood days at our home
All the family together, oh, the joys I have known.
No T.V.s, computers or 'lectronic toys,
The evenings at home were a blessing and joy.
After supper we took turns to wash and dry dishes,
Then clear off the table with mom's good wishes,
And then to the parlor, sliding doors fast in place,
Out of bounds 'cept on Sunday
And our evenings of grace.
We'd all gather round as dad read us the stories
From the books in the Bible
That tell of God's glories.
Mom would play the piano,
Dad would lead us in hymns,
Praising Jesus our Savior
Who has burdened our sins,
Mom and dad now have gone
To their home up above
But my memories remain of
our home filled with love.

– ALBERT N. THEEL

Part One

The Lawrence Till family, 1937, on their farm north of Fort Wayne Indiana. From left to right, top to bottom (top row), Jimmy, Dorothy, Pauline, Rita, Lawrence, Kathleen, (bottom row) Mary Ann, Jane, Herman, Paul and Terrie.

THIS IS A BOOK ABOUT MY CHILDHOOD BEGINNING WITH MY EARLIEST memory. It is for my children and grandchildren. Though I don't really remember being born, I do know I was born at home April 8, 1936. Named Dorothy Agnes Till. I was the ninth child of Lawrence and Pauline Till. We lived on a farm just four miles north of Fort Wayne Indiana. In 1936, my oldest brother, Jimmy, was already away from home going to school at a seminary studying to be a priest, and my sister Terrie had just contracted Polio and was in a hospital in Indianapolis. My two oldest sisters, Kate and Rita, were also no longer living at home as both had left for a convent school at age fourteen. The rest of my siblings, in order of age – Herman, Teresa, Mary Ann, Paul and Jane – were still at home when I arrived.

*Paul,
Dorothy
and Jane.*

*Baby Dorothy,
Paul and Jane.*

My parents told me that I could walk and talk at eight months old. They said I could speak whole sentences. For instance, I would point to the door and say "opie doe."

I remember one time when I was small my mother wanted me to take a nap. But I didn't want to take a nap, so I hid. They found me later asleep under the old oil stove that was up on legs.

We used to have a little housedog in those days. Mom would hold the dog and I would hide. Then she would let the dog loose to find me.

*Our dog taking
Kitty for a ride.*

*Dorothy Agnes
with bow in hair.*

I remember the other children all went off to school everyday on the big yellow school bus. My mother sometimes would fix me a little lunch in a brown paper bag so that I could pretend to be going to school also. I really wanted to go to kindergarten, but living in the country we didn't have kindergarten. Being five years old, I thought kindergarten was pronounced "Henry's garden," so I used to get my doll and pretend I went to Henry's garden and there I would eat my snack.

Dorothy Agnes on her first day of school.

I can still remember the first day at school in first grade. My mom had made me a pink organdy dress with flowers embroidered on it with a pink bonnet to match. It must have been just too cute. But someone made fun of it on the bus, and I cried most of all the first day at school.

I'll never forget the odor that big yellow school bus had. Most everyone brought their lunches. And some ate part of it on the way to school. It had a strong aroma of orange peels and egg salad and bologna sandwiches. Once in awhile mom would let us buy our lunch at school. It wasn't a favorite thing for me. Our first grade teacher wouldn't let us go to recess until we at least tasted everything on our plate. I remember missing a whole lunch break because I wouldn't try the horrible canned spinach on my plate.

Lawrence and Pauline on their wedding day on June 5, 1920 with Thomas Till and Mary Spires.

We lived just a little under a mile to church. It was a small Catholic church. There were only a few families that attended it. But the families were huge. Our family consisted of my mom and dad and nine children. My dad's family had nine boys and one girl. And most of my uncles and their families lived close by so there were quite a few Tills that went to that church and a huge family of Ryans and Boobys.

In May of second grade I made my first communion. About a month before I was to make my first confession and first communion, Mary Ann drew a picture of a garden with cut out flowers and weeds. Everyday that I was good she would put a flower in the garden. And if I did something bad she put a weed in it.

My sisters and I often walked to church in the spring and summer time. It was fun to pick wild flowers on the way home. I remember walking to church in the winter one time, when the snow was up to our knees. We had no choice but to walk because the cars couldn't travel the roads. We didn't have big snowplows like they do now. In the wintertime we would listen to the radio in the morning to see what schools were closed because of the weather. When they announced "Washington School," which is the one we attended, we would jump up and down and prepare for a fun day at home.

Daasy Agnes.

When we were growing up there was a boy at our church, Mary Ann's age, about five years older than me. He used to always call me "Daasy Agnes" (Dah-see Agnes). I just hated it then. But now that I'm older I think it's kind of cute. That's how my book got its name. ✺

Part Two

Skating on our neighbor's pond.

WE HAD OUR CHOICE OF A COUPLE DIFFERENT PLACES TO ICE SKATE depending on how much rain we got that year. There was always skating in a neighbors swamp in the woods. We would skate in between trees. It was such a glorious site after a big snow. The tree branches were full of snow and we had the whole area to ourselves –my siblings, cousins and a few friends. We used to go skating almost every evening after school if the pond was frozen. We always stayed too long. By the time we started home, which was probably about a quarter of a mile away, our fingers and toes would be frostbitten. I can remember just lying down in the snow and crying for the pain in my fingers and toes and then getting back up and trudging on home. When we got home, we would go to the sinks and tub and run water over our extremities until the numbness subsided. But we would go back and do the same thing again the next day.

Our creek in the winter.

We used to go to the pond at nighttime too. The boys would build a big bonfire of logs right on the ice for light and to keep warm. We played our own make shift hockey with our homemade sticks and pucks. Mom would have popcorn and hot chocolate drinks for us when we got home.

We didn't have a television when we were growing up. We pretty much had to entertain ourselves. There was a story telling radio station that came on after school everyday, called "Marmaduke the Book Worm." I used to lay on the floor with my eyes closed and listen to those stories.

Jane and Daasy Agnes with dolls.

On Saturdays we all had our chores to do. The girls chores consisted mostly of cleaning the house. Our older sisters Mary Ann and Terrie would tell Jane and I that if we got our work done by one o'clock that they would play paper dolls with us. We did have some paper dolls that came from the store, but our favorite thing to do was to make our own dolls and all their clothes. We spent the first hour or so by ourselves drawing our dolls and making their clothes. Then we would get together and pretend the dolls were going to school, church, parties and other places and dress them for the occasions. It was so much fun to create outfits for our dolls of our own colors choices and styles and designs. I remember one time, just to be different, I made all of my doll's clothes pink and chartreuse.

Mary Ann was especially creative and artistic. She used to write plays for us. She would cast us in the parts and we would practice all day sometimes. When she thought we were good enough, we would put the plays on for mom and dad and Herman and Paul or whoever was around but not in the plays. To make a stage, we would string a thin rope across the living room and hang sheets on it for the curtains.

MaryAnn, Jane and Dorothy.

Margaret O'Brien was a popular child actress at the time and I used to try to imitate her. One time Mary Anne and Jane and I put on a play about Terrie and her boy friends. Jane would dress up in different clothes and pretend to be a variety of Terrie's boyfriends. I played the part of Terrie. When one boyfriend knocked on the door for a date, I (Terrie) answered the door with my hair in curlers wearing a short skirt with snuggies (underpants) showing underneath. Our mom and dad had such a laugh over this. But Terrie was not amused.

Dorothy, Jane and Paul working on the farm, September 1946.

One of our favorite summertime games was kick the can. Our cousins, Uncle Al and Aunt Angeline's family, were some of our closest neighbors. There were seven boys and the youngest was a girl. The two oldest boys' names were Bill and Louie. So we always called that family the Bill Louies. We'd play kick the can with the Bill Louies. There were always at least a half dozen of us. We would throw a baseball bat to see who had to be the first to hide their eyes. Everyone put one hand on top of the others and whoever's hand was on the top of the bat had to close their eyes while holding onto a tree and someone would draw on their back saying, "I'll draw the frying pan and who'll put the sausage in?" Someone else then would touch his back. If he guessed who it was, that person had to hide his eyes. Otherwise the first person had to count to 100 and then warn everyone that he was coming ready or not. And then he would go hunt everyone. If he found someone and ran back and touched the can before the person whom he found did, that person would be out. If he was looking for someone and someone else ran in and kicked the can, then everyone could hide again. And the same person had to count to 100 and start all over.

*Terrie in front of
our corn shed.*

We had lots of hiding places. One of my favorites was on top of the milk shed that was between the barn and the corn shed. We'd run behind the corn shed and climb up the slats of the corn shed and onto the top of the milk shed. That would give a pretty good overview of where everyone else was hiding. But if you were spotted it wasn't likely that you would have time to kick the can. We would usually play until it got almost dark.

Paul on tractor.

Our farm was a small family farm. My parents owned about 50 acres. But dad farmed over 100 acres. He farmed a neighbor's farm, Mosey. Mosey owned a sporting good and game shop in town. Mosey always remembered the Till kids on Christmas. He brought us games from his store and always a big sack of red delicious apples and a huge box of heath-like bars of candy for us. Dad always kept the box of candy in his and mom's bedroom in one of his drawers in their dresser. He would let us each have a piece of candy once a day. But we used to sneak in and take a piece once in awhile. I know he had to know that we did this but he never said anything.

Dad working the fields on the wagon.

Uncle John, Cousin Frank, and Lawrence (dad) bailing hay.

On the farm, we had two workhorses, Dick and Prince. We always had about a dozen or so milk cows. We had a lot of pigs, I'd guess about forty or so, and lots and lots of chickens and usually only a few roosters. We always had one dog and a few cats. In our big red barn there were two hay lofts. There was a ladder that went up to the top of the barn on the inside in one of those haylofts.

Morning on the farm was announced by the rooster.

Jane and Daasy Agnes on haystack.

We used to climb to the top of the ladder and jump into the hay stack. Then when we got brave, we used to try and do a somersault on the way down. I remember one time when I hit the hay I passed out temporarily. No one told mom because we didn't want to get into trouble.

Playing tiger on the barn rafters.

Jane, Paul and I used to play tiger. Paul was always the tiger and he'd chase Jane and I. We would all be on the high beams in the barn. I remember I used to be as scared as if he was a real tiger. When I look back at this it isn't even funny. If we would have fallen off those beams we would have been seriously injured or dead. Mom never knew about that one either.

Daasy Agnes on her tricycle.

Our heating system for our two-story farm house was a coal furnace. The huge furnace and a coal bin were in one area of the basement and in another area we kept the chicken eggs. There was also a huge potato bin and a large area where mom kept all her home canned goods. Under the steps dad had a few vats of dandelion wine that he made.

We all took turns shoveling the coal into the furnace. Mary Ann, Jane and I used to have fun doing it. While we were shoveling coal in the cold winter, we would sing. We thought we harmonized but the truth is I don't think any of us carried a tune very well. Our favorite song was "The weather out side is frightful, but the fire is so delightful, so since there's no place to go, let it snow, let it snow, let it snow."

The heat circulated through the house by floor registers. There was one register in most of the rooms. Dad used to set mouse traps in the registers. I thought the mice were so cute, and I used to put little pieces of cheese around for the mice in the registers. When mom and dad found out, of course, it had to stop. But they did have a sense of humor about it. And I got a toy mouse that year for Christmas.

Jane, Paul and Dorothy.

When I was little, there were just two rooms upstairs, which later were made into three rooms and an upstairs bathroom. The boys were in one room and the girls in the other.

We had two beds in the girls' room, two girls to each bed. Some mornings in the winter it was so cold. The first one up turned on the light. There was one light that hung down from a cord in the middle of the room. That person would run to the register and stand there and put on their clothes and throw everyone else's clothes to them, so we could put our clothes on under the covers.

Mom and Dad's 40th Wedding Anniversary. Front: Herman, Jimmy, MaryLynn (Rita's daughter), Paul. Back: Terrie, Dorothy, Dad, Mom, Sister Kate, Rita, Jame.

Our social life consisted of family get-togethers, church and school. Our church had a few events every year that everyone went to. I remember an evening we had a chicken and noodle dinner and played Bingo afterwards.

Dorothy with hat on at the side of the house.

Every year in the summer, we had an all day social with food and entertainment and games. One game that the kids were allowed to work at was the fish game. It consisted of a four-sided tent-like construction without a top. It cost ten cents to play the game. The player would throw the fishing pole's line into the tent and the workers inside would attach a gift to the line, and the player would reel in the gift. I was old enough to work in the tent at the time, probably about seven or eight. While working in the tent I spotted this beautiful glass picture of Jesus that was one of the prizes. I wanted it so much I stole it. The worst part was that I had to confess the sin in confession. And I'm sure the parish priest knew exactly who I was. I don't remember how many Hail Mary's I had to say for penance, but I do know I started putting dimes in the collection box.

Daasy Agnes with Teddy bear and Jane with Judy doll .

Being the youngest child, I probably had more toys than anyone else in the family. But we girls all got one good doll. I named my doll Teresa Doll and Jane named her doll Judy Doll. Many years later Ted and I would have our own real Judy Doll, plus Sam, Tom and Joe dolls.

"Eliza Jane with her Easter dress on"

Dorothy Bergaul

Our family wasn't prejudiced, although I can't remember any blacks in our community. And I don't remember how this all came about without TV or any real influence but I always wanted a black doll. Back in the Post WWII days things like that weren't really very available. So that Christmas mom made me a black raggedy Ann doll. I was so thrilled with the doll. I called her Eliza Jane.

I loved my Eliza Jane. I used to hide in the attic or in back of a huge closet with a light in it, and sew by hand, dresses for my Eliza Jane. Every holiday I would bring Eliza Jane out to show everyone her new outfit. One Christmas I made her a red dress with matching socks and hat. And one Easter I made her a yellow dress. I embroidered flowers and leaves on it. And it even had a collar with lace that I had tatted.

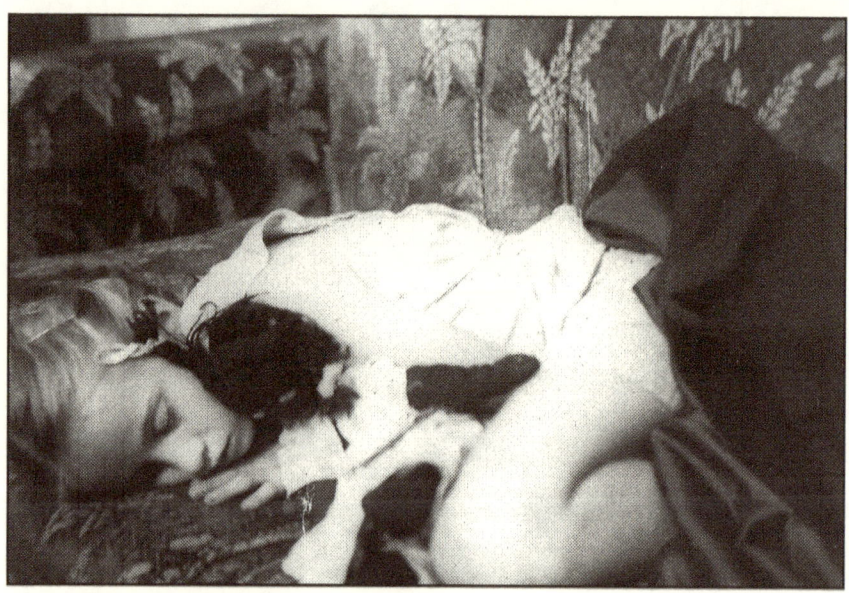

My mother had taught me how to tat. I don't know if it's a lost art or if people still do it. It was done with a small instrument that you feed the string into and manipulate the thread to make lace. The lace we made wasn't real fancy, but we used it as border for pillows cases and other items. My enthusiasm for Eliza Jane caught on. For Christmas she started to get gifts from my family, like ice skates and roller skates and other cute items.

Our wood stove that burned through the winter.

The old wood stove in the kitchen was used mainly in the wintertime. The oil stove was used in the summer, because it wasn't as hot as the wood stove. The wood stove had a place that you put the wood, burners on top and a vent that went outside to a chimney. It also had an oven with a place to keep water heated. We would dip the water out of the stoves for our baths.

We had a sink in the kitchen that had a pump and handle. Someone had to pump the handle to get the cold water from the well. As kids we used to sit up on the sink and wash our feet at night before we went to bed. I don't remember when we got hot running water. Probably after World War II.

Dan and Teresa Fox's home where Pauline (mom) was born.

Pauline's childhood home on Stony Hill Road near Lancaster, Ohio. The picture was taken on August 18, 1984, many years after the home was renovated.

We had an old fashion bathtub that was up on claws. We also had an outside bathroom called an outhouse, and we kept an old Sears and Roebuck catalog in the outhouse, using the pages for toilet paper. Dad always used to say, "those darn girls," because he never got a turn to go in the inside bathroom. The girls were always in there primping.

Mom husking corn in the backyard.

Every year there was a contest for farmers. I'm not sure who sponsored it, whether it was the Farm Bureau or 4H. Dad used to always enter the contest for his corn, and got first prize just about every year. He would take an almost perfect ear of corn and carefully take any less than perfect kernels out and glue perfect ones in their place. That might be considered cheating, but it was also pretty clever. ☞

Part Three

When I was in the fourth grade I became very ill that winter, sometime after the holidays. All I knew was that I had a very sore throat and Dr. McCardle, our family doctor, made a home visit to come see me.

I never was told exactly what was wrong with me. But from what I know now, I would guess it started out as a strept throat and got into my blood stream. The doctor said I would have to have my tonsils out, but first I would have to be hospitalized to get rid of the infection. I was very, very ill. The doctors even warned my parents that they didn't know if I would live.

Penicillin was a very knew drug then. It was invented during WWII from extract of mold and was just being released for civilian use. I remember getting those big penicillin shots in my bottom around the clock. I even received part of a blood transfusion that my dad donated, but I had an allergic reaction to it, so it was stopped. It seems that I was in the hospital about five days before they took my tonsils out.

I remember those days in the hospital as if it were yesterday. I remember I could see a huge sign advertising John Deere tractors from the sixth floor pediatric room.

I made friends with the other children. There was one boy that used to visit me at meal time in his wheel chair. He always ate my Jello and custards and puddings. It's too late to know now, but I bet those nurses thought that I ate that food. Little did I know that some years after that I would graduate from that same hospital as an RN (Registered Nurse).

Terrie and Herman.

Terrie came up to see me one time and brought Eliza Jane, thinking that it would cheer me up. But at age nine with my new friends there, I was embarrassed and hid her under my pillow.

I missed a month of school that year in the fourth grade due to my illness and my fourth grade teacher told my parents that she would have to hold me back because I missed a lot of English grammar and mathematics.

After leaving the hospital, I had a couple of weeks recovery at home. My mother, who was so devoted and such a good nurse, was always there for me. She knew I was bored so to keep me entertained she taught me how to sew. I made two tiny rag dolls about five inches long. I called them Scratchy and Itchy. I ended up making about three more, but don't remember their names. I wish I would have kept them.

Little by little I recovered. I still recall the first day I went out doors. It had all of a sudden turned into a spring day, and Jane wanted me to play

jump rope with her. We used to tie one end of the rope to a pillar on the porch and one person would swing it while the other one jumped. Each time raising it a little higher until that person missed then she had to hold the rope. Jane could jump higher than anyone at school; she had the longest legs. Jane always waited for a car to go by when she jumped, so the people in the car could see her.

Mom and dad took me to school on my first day back since my illness. Mrs. Foster gave me a big hug. Evidently I caught up with my class. I wasn't kept back and got to go onto fifth grade with my classmates.

In the fifth grade, our teacher let us listen to the World Series base ball games on the radio right during regular classroom time. We were all big baseball, basketball and football fans in those days. Even though we didn't have TV, we listened to them on the radio.

THE NEWS-SENTINEL, FORT WAYNE, INDIAN...

Olympic Preview A...

Joe Louis Still Confident He Will Become Champion

Returns To Mat Here Wednesd...

BULLETIN

HAMBURG, Germany, July 4—(I.N.S.)—Max Schmeling today dealt a deadly right to schemes for a return bout with Joe Louis before the German gets a chance to win back the championship.

"I don't care about the possible money in another Louis fight," he said, "I insist on a match with Braddock in September."

BY PAT ROBINSON

NEW YORK, July 4—(I.N.S.)—Joe Louis still believes he can lick any man in the world, Max Schmeling and Jim Braddock included, and expects to be champion of the world by next June.

...radio broadcast which netted him $1,250 for a few minutes ...expressed his eagerness to meet any and all comers ...times to fight at least once a month. ..." said Joe, referring to his five ...nout me

Mom and Dad didn't go out very often in the evening, especially during the week. But one time they went out on a weekday evening, and Herman and his friend Jay and all the rest of us decided to play "Murder in the Dark." The only problem was that I had all this math homework to get done. Herman who was a real brain and later would become high school salutatorian and graduate magnum cum laude from Notre Dame, said he would do my math for me so I could play "Murder in the Dark" with them.

The rules of the game "Murder in the Dark" were that someone was the murderer and was "It," the one that counted to 100 while everyone else hid. All the lights in the house were turned off, and we could hide anywhere in the house, which consisted of the basement, ground floor and upstairs. The person who was "It" had to find and touch each person in the dark, and if you were touched, it meant that you were murdered until everyone was found. It was really scary. I remember hiding up high on a closet shelf. That's all I recall of the game. But I'll never forget the next day when I handed in my math homework, all the answers were wrong. I learned my lesson about letting someone else do my homework no matter how smart they are.

Rita didn't stay in the convent. She and Herman went into town to the Catholic high school (Central Catholic). Rita and Herman sat at a card table every evening to do their homework, while the rest of us were either in the kitchen or upstairs. One time while studying, Rita kept making these snort like noises. It really irritated Herman. Dad looked in and could tell that Herman was really agitated. Dad said, "What's going on in there?" and Herman said, "Rita's breathing."

Herman and Mary Ann.

There was a small town a few miles away named Leo. Every Tuesday night in the summer the town would show free out door movies. The movies were older black and white movies that were no longer in the theaters. Dad always told us if we did all our chores that day, we'd get to go to the Leo shows. Sometimes we would go early and we'd stop at a quarry on the way. It was so clear you could see every pebble on the bottom. Dad and the boys would go swimming. I don't think the girls ever went. We used to all get a treat of an ice cream cone on that night out. My favorite flavor was strawberry --it was out of this world. We would bring blankets and sit on them in the empty lot and watch the movie. It wasn't like a drive-in movie. It was just a large screen and a projector.

When cows have calves, they become very overly protective of their offspring. They become just like a bull. They don't want anyone around their calf. Usually all of our cows were out to pasture all day. At the end of the day, a couple of us and the dog would go get them and bring them back to the barn for milking.

One afternoon I went down past the gate into the area where another barn and chicken coop were. A cow that had a calf was there with her calf. She was supposed to be in the pasture with the other cows. She saw me and started to run, charging toward me. I ran into the open doored barn and climbed the ladder to the loft. She stood at the stairs and snorted and snorted and stomped her feet at me. She wouldn't leave. I had to spend the rest of the day up in the loft until dad came home from the field. I can't recall what he did to tame her but I made it down from the loft.

Our schoolyard in grade school was quite large. I would guess that it was about five acres. I know all the classes from fourth to eighth grade had their own baseball fields. This was a country school and it must have been back to back with some farm or someone's private property because at one end of the schoolyard, there was an electrical fence with barbed wire. One time at recess, about twenty of us lined up and held hands in a row. The first person touched the electric wire, and the electricity went through us one by one down the line and out the last person's hand. I don't believe any teachers knew about that. And we didn't tell mom that one either.

During the summer time, we would sometimes sleep outside under the stars. I remember one summer there were a number of reports that people had spotted a huge snake in the country close to where we lived. The mystery snake was soon named Pete the Python. One night a friend, Jeannine, Jane and I slept outdoors under a crescent moon. After Jane fell asleep, Jeannine and I snuck back in the house and left Jane alone outside. When she woke up, she was so mad at us because Pete the Python could have taken her away.

The family game that we played in the summer time was croquet. I still remember how pretty the yard looked in the summer with the peonies and roses in bloom.

One game we played as kids was "Mother May I." One person would be in charge and the others would line up on one side of the yard. The one in charge would tell each person to take two baby steps or two giant steps or some other combination of steps. The challenge was to see who could get to the other side first. One could sneak steps in between being told. If you got caught or didn't do exactly what the one in charge said, you had to go back to the start. If you didn't get caught, you could sneak across first. Jane always cheated in this game.

Part Four

Jimmy

WHEN WE WERE KIDS AND WORLD WAR II WAS STILL GOING ON, THE government strongly urged us to invest in war bonds. Another thing they asked was for everyone to look for anything rubber (like old rubber tires) and anything made of tin like chewing gum wrappers. They used the tin by balling it up and throwing it out the windows of our fighter planes over the enemy's planes to interfere with their radars so they wouldn't know where to drop their bombs.

Dad used to have two mallard ducks on the farm that he had tamed. One fall day a couple of city folks asked dad if they could hunt on his farm, and dad said yes.

They came back at the end of the day with these two mallard ducks they had shot. Dad told them that they were his pets. The guys felt real bad about it and gave them to the family to eat. Later dad found some duck eggs along the creek, so he put the eggs in a nest for a banty hen to sit on until they hatched. If you aren't familiar with banty hens, they are real small, about half the size of a regular chicken, and are reddish brown. The banty hen dutifully sat on the eggs until they hatched. I think she was a little surprised to see that she produced ducks.

Dad made a little swimming area for the ducks out of an old sink. The ducks immediately went in for a swim. The banty hen couldn't figure that one out either. In no time at all, the four ducks got to be about twice the size of the banty. But they always followed her around in a line. Later in my life when I was married and had my own four teenagers, I would take them all shopping for school clothes in the fall. My children all were so much taller than me. It made me feel like the banty hen being followed by the big ducks.

Paul riding Prince.

When the workhorses, Dick and Prince, weren't out in the field working, Jane and I, and sometimes a friend or two, would spend hours sitting on them in the stable just talking girl things. One day Jane and I had this brainstorm to ride them. We rode out of the stable and onto the gravel drive way. Dick and Prince immediately reared up and threw us both off. We got a little scratched up, but weren't hurt badly. I found out later that workhorses are not supposed to be tamed and ridden.

Every evening after supper, when the cows were milked and the dishes done, our whole family would gather in the living room and get down on our knees and say the family rosary. Sometimes mom would lead and sometimes dad would lead. Us girls had a hard time not snickering through the rosary when dad led. He would say the Hail Mary about half in German and half in English.

We had a piano at home when we grew up. Mom played really well. She taught us little pieces, but I guess she didn't have time to give us real lessons. Our sister Terrie played the violin real well. She later became the first violinist in the high school orchestra. Some evenings mom would play the piano and Terrie the violin and we would all sing along. We didn't have TV in those days, so we had to entertain ourselves. It was great not having TV when we grew up. It gave us a lot more time to be creative.

*Uncle John working the
threshing machine.*

*Uncle Tom catching wheat from the
threshing machine with a burlap bag.*

*Uncles John and
Leo, Dad, my
cousins, uncle Al,
and my brother
Paul cutting wood.*

Every summer on the farm we threshed. Dad's brothers, also living on farms near by, all pitched in and helped each other thresh. The big machine, called the Threshing Machine, picked straw from the field and separated it from the grain. It had a big funnel that blew straw into a big stack called a straw stack and separated the wheat or oats into a bin. Once the straw stack settled in, the kids would climb up the straw stack and slide down.

Grandfather Daniel Fox, my mom's sister Mary & neighbor in front of the family's famous silo.

My grandfather built the first silo ever seen in that part of the world. He was very proud of it. He had read that this new invention would be a great help in preserving food for his cattle during the winter months.

My cousins Jerry and Harold, Terrie, Jane and me.

    The wives would get together and cook a huge meal for the threshers, who always got to eat first. The wives and kids would eat only after the threshers had finished. After lunch, the kids would get to help the threshers clean up, which was way more fun than doing all those dishes.

My uncles cutting wood.

Thanksgiving day was the day that the farmers would pick horse corn. We never celebrated Thanksgiving because it was a big workday for farmers. We always had our Thanksgiving dinner with turkey on Christmas day.

We would all go to midnight mass on Christmas eve. Mom would get up early, about 4:30 AM, and put the turkey in the oven for our Christmas dinner. We would open our gifts when we got up.

Uncle John.

Uncle Tom and uncle John, our two bachelor uncles always came for Christmas dinner. Uncle John was a farmer and always gave each of us kids 50 cents every year. Uncle Tom, an architect, always gave us each a dollar. In those days we thought it to be a great and generous gift.

Uncle Leo.

The farmers had a machine called a corn shredder that would pick the corn stalk and all, and shred it all up into what they called fodder. This is what they fed to their stock, cows and horses.

The corn fed to chickens was different. That corn was picked by hand, put into a wagon and transported to the corn shed, then shelled by hand. Later on we got a shelling machine, which was much easier than shelling it by hand.

Paul on our tractor.

As kids, we always had our daily chores. The girls' chores mainly consisted of feeding the chickens and gathering the eggs. In the wintertime, we also had to bring in wood for the wood stove.

The boys' chores where to help on the farm, bringing the cows in, feeding the cows and pigs and horses, and helping milk the cows. We all took turns going out to the field with the dog to bring the cows in to be milked.

Terrie.

My sister Jane learned to milk the cows even though it really wasn't considered a girl's job. Mom milked the cows too. Later on, dad got a milking machine. They used to have a radio on playing music when they milked the cows. They thought it helped the cows give milk. We usually had nine to eleven cows, and had names for all of them. My favorite one was called Rhoney.

In the Midwest before it rains, especially on a farm, the flies get real pesty. We used to get hundreds of them on the front porch screen. Of course, some would get into the house. Mom would give all of us fly swatters, and give us a penny for each fly we killed.

Dorothy.

After the war, many things were rationed, due to the shortage of supplies. Gas and tires were rationed, and also sugar, which made bubble gum rationed too. A couple of the older kids used to walk about two miles to the closest little country store to buy bubble gum. They were only allowed one piece of gum per person. When they brought it home, Mom made us take turns sharing the gum. She would boil it in between each person. The old saying about leaving your gum on the bedpost over night probably had some truth to it.

Lawrence Till
(dad).

Dad used to go fishing every Sunday after church with his brothers, a pal, or his boys. Mom never went, and he never took the girls. In the winter, he would go ice fishing, and almost always caught his limit.

Sunday was mom's day to stay home and write letters. She always said she was perfectly content to do that. She would also fix a huge Sunday dinner that included a great dessert, usually a home baked pie. Dad always wanted a dessert with every meal, even lunch.

My father's parents, Henry and Ellen (Judy) Till on their wedding in 1853.

Henry and Ellen Till.

Henry and Ellen Till with Uncle Joe.

Grandma Till, Dad's mom used to bake ten pies every Saturday. By Sunday evening they all would be gone.

There was a popular song during the war sung by the Andrew Sisters called "Don't Sit Under the Apple Tree". The words were, "Don't sit under the apple tree with anyone else but me until I come marching home."

World War II ended in 1945. We heard about it on the radio, and celebrated by running out in the front yard throwing rags in the air. When the rags settled and the troops did at last come marching home, life on the farm began to change quickly for me, and many years later, I found someone to sit with under the apple tree.

About the Author

This is Dorothy Burgards first book. Dorothy was born in 1936. At the outbreak of World War II she was 4 yrs. old. Dorothy is a registered nurse and a watercolor artist. She is married. They have four children and five grandchildren. She lives in Southern California with her husband.

www.ingramcontent.com/pod-product-compliance
Lightning Source LLC
Chambersburg PA
CBHW020410290526
45785CB00005B/2502